Rainforests at Risk

Alison Hawes

Contents

ZAC'S JOURNAL

Zac Trotter
Aged 11

4th May

I have been home for a week now with my leg in plaster (my skateboard had an argument with a lamp post!) and already I'm totally bored!

I've spent hours on the computer or watching TV and I've even done all my school work. Well, okay, not all of it - I have one piece of writing left to do but I haven't decided what to write about yet. BORED! BORED! BORED!

Me in hospital

Joel
(My brother)

Reema
(My cousin)

Ruth
(My sister)

5th May

I've received loads of Get Well cards but only one Get Well letter. It arrived this morning from my Uncle Jim Trotter or 'Globe' Trotter (ha! ha!), as I like to call him. Globe is an explorer and a conservationist. He has a bedroom in our house but he's hardly ever there! In fact, he was on his way to South America when he sent me this ...

Somewhere over
the Atlantic Ocean
28th April

Hi Zac,

I'm on my flight to Brazil. To pass the time on the plane, I'm catching up on emails and writing letters. So here is my Get Well letter to you!

Your Dad tells me you've broken your leg, so I thought I'd set you a little challenge to keep you occupied (and away from your games console!) while you're stuck at home.

I'm flying out to Brazil to take part in an expedition to the Amazon rainforest. We're going to be studying how the animals and people of the area share the rainforest.

The first part of your challenge is to work out why the rainforest is home to so many different animals. The enclosed book about the rainforest should help you work out the answer.

I'll email you in a few days to see how you're getting on.

Good luck!

Globe

P.S. I have a great outing in mind for you, as a reward, if you manage to complete the challenge.

Reward Clue 1: It's something to do with animals.

I was so pleased to have something new to do,
I opened the book Globe had sent straight away ...

Rainforests Rule!

Unique places

Rainforests are some of the most important places on the planet because:

- They are home to more **species** of plant and animal than anywhere else in the world!
- They provide the Earth with two things we cannot do without: water and oxygen.
- They are a source of food and medicines.
- They provide a home for many people.

Find it!
The biggest rainforest in the world is 25 times bigger than the UK! Can you find it on the map?

NORTH AMERICA

EUROPE

ASIA

AFRICA

EQUATOR

N

SOUTH AMERICA

AUSTRALIA

E

S

KEY
RAINFORESTS

There are many different kinds of rainforest but almost all of them are found in the tropics – the areas of the world closest to the **equator** – where it is hot and rainy all year round.

Lowland forests

Most tropical rainforests are lowland forests. Here the land is fairly flat and the tree growth thick and tall. This is because the warm, wet atmosphere in lowland rainforests is absolutely perfect for trees and plants to grow.

In the clouds

Montane rainforests are found where rainforest trees grow on hills and mountain sides.

It is cooler and damper here than in lowland rainforests and the trees are often shorter and hidden in thick mist or fog, which is why these forests are sometimes also known as cloud forests. Moss and ferns love these moist conditions and grow thickly on the trees.

On stilts

The trees in mangrove rainforests look as if they are growing on stilts! They grow in areas where the rainforest meets the sea.

Their roots grow high above the water, keeping the tree trunks and leaves away from the salty water that would normally kill most plants.

So what is it about lowland rainforest that makes it such a perfect place for plants to grow?
Globe

The Amazon Rainforest

World's largest

The largest continuous area of rainforest in the world is the Amazon rainforest. This massive rainforest, of six million square kilometres, covers 40 per cent of South America! It is a really important place as it produces more than 20 per cent of the Earth's oxygen. That is why some call it the 'Lungs of the Planet'.

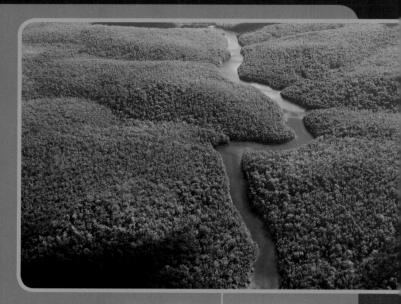

Through the heart of this rainforest runs the mighty Amazon River.

How much of the Amazon rainforest is in each country?

PERU
BRAZIL
BOLIVIA
COLOMBIA
ECUADOR — OTHER COUNTRIES

The Amazon rainforest stretches into nine different countries.

Find it!

Most of the Amazon rainforest lies in which country?

Amazon River facts

- It is over 6400 km long.
- Over 200 other rivers flow into it.
- It holds a fifth of the world's fresh water.
- It is home to over 2000 different types of fish .
- It is the second longest river in the world.

Hot and steamy

The Amazon rainforest is a lowland tropical rainforest, so the climate is usually warm and **humid**. An enormous variety of trees and plants grows happily in this atmosphere and they, in turn, provide food and shelter for a wide variety of animals and birds.

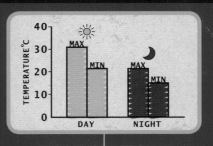

Temperatures are high in the forest all year round.

Rainfall

About 2000 mm of rain falls in the Amazon rainforest every year. That's about three times the rain that London gets every year. So you can see how *rain*forests got their name! The rains falls mostly in the afternoons, often in short sharp bursts. It can take up to ten minutes for the rain to reach the forest floor, because the **canopy** of trees is so thick!

Can you think of two reasons why a huge variety of plants attracts a wide variety of animals and birds?
Globe

Flooded out!

Most rain falls during the wet season, when rivers can burst and many areas of the forest become flooded for months at a time. In the dry season, only about 110 000 square km of the forest is covered by water compared to up to 350 000 square km in the wet season!

Rainforest Layers

Tropical rainforests have five distinct layers. Each layer provides a habitat for different animals and plants.

Emergent Layer

The few trees that are tall enough to rise above the rainforest canopy form what is known as the emergent layer. These trees get more sun and wind than any other layer of the forest. Trees, such as the kapok tree and Brazil nut tree, are found here and can grow up to 70 m high. This habitat suits many birds.

Canopy

Most of the trees in the rainforest grow very close to one another. These trees form such a dense canopy, they act like a giant umbrella, leaving the ground below in deep shade. Bigger animals like monkeys and sloths like living up here.

Water

On some stretches of water, you will see **submerged** tree roots. On others, you might see giant water lilies with huge flat leaves over a metre across and massive flowers as big as footballs! Fish, river dolphins and land animals that can swim can be found in and around water.

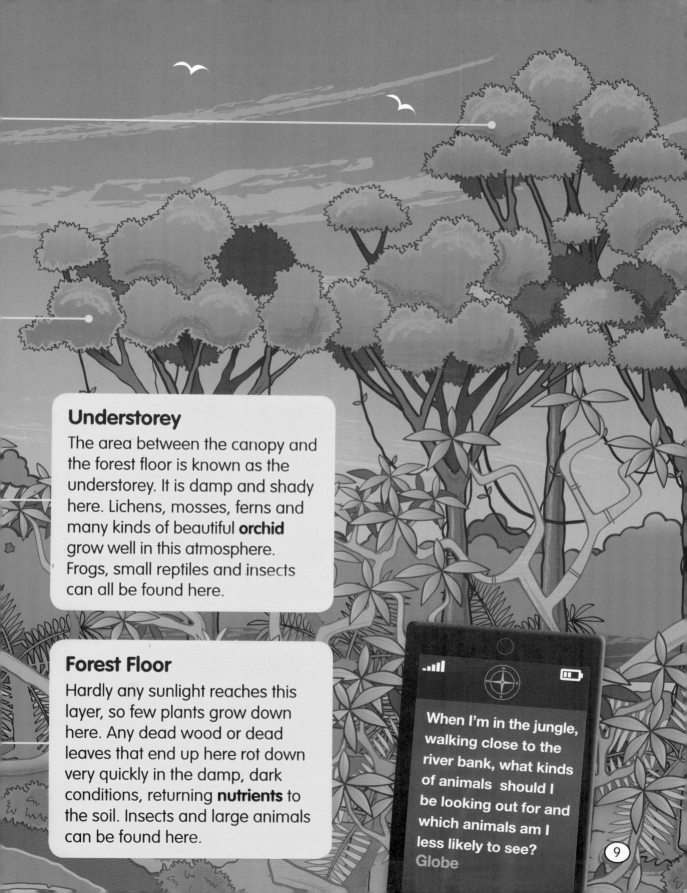

Understorey

The area between the canopy and the forest floor is known as the understorey. It is damp and shady here. Lichens, mosses, ferns and many kinds of beautiful **orchid** grow well in this atmosphere. Frogs, small reptiles and insects can all be found here.

Forest Floor

Hardly any sunlight reaches this layer, so few plants grow down here. Any dead wood or dead leaves that end up here rot down very quickly in the damp, dark conditions, returning **nutrients** to the soil. Insects and large animals can be found here.

When I'm in the jungle, walking close to the river bank, what kinds of animals should I be looking out for and which animals am I less likely to see?
Globe

9

INTO THE JUNGLE

6th May

Why I think so many animals live in the rainforest

- The climate in the rainforest is just right for lots of different plants and trees to grow.
- Plant-eating animals, birds and insects that eat the roots, shoots, leaves or fruit of the different plants and trees come to feed and shelter in the rainforest.
- Animals and birds that eat these animals, birds and insects come to feed and shelter in the rainforest too.

7th May

Globe's just emailed me to find out whether I'd worked out yet, why rainforests are home to so many different animals. Wow - I'd already written about that yesterday!

I think he was surprised that I emailed him back almost immediately with my answer. He obviously didn't realise how bored I was (ha! ha!).

Zac

From: Globetrotter
To: Zac Trotter
Sent: 10th May 8:22
Subject: Challenge

Hi Zac,
Wow! That was quick! Well done for completing the first part of the challenge. Now for the next part: I need you to find out all you can about the animals in the rainforest and make a list of your top five most dangerous. (Just imagine it was you going on an expedition, rather than me. Which animals would you be keen to avoid?)

This is me about to head off into the Amazonian rainforest. I probably look a bit overdressed in my hat and long sleeves but I need them to keep the insects at bay! I'll email you in a few days or so, when we next reach somewhere with an internet connection.

Globe

P.S.
Reward Clue 2: If you complete the challenge, you are going to need a torch.

Globe's second clue about the reward has puzzled me. I just can't think what it's going to be, but the sooner I continue the challenge the sooner I'll know, I suppose! So I'm going to look up the section on rainforest animals in the book he sent, right now ...

Emergent Trees and the Canopy

Up in the trees

Hundreds of different animals live high up in the rainforest trees. Some will spend their whole life up there without ever coming down to ground level, because all the food and shelter they need is there.

Up in the canopy, you will find butterflies, frogs and lizards, as well as many of the rainforest's larger animals such as birds, monkeys and sloths.

Spiderman moves

Spider monkeys are ideally suited to living in trees. They have slender limbs and a long tail which help them to climb, jump and swing through the canopy like a miniature Spiderman! They have been known to travel ten metres in a single leap!

Spider monkeys use their long tails as an extra hand.

Top predator

Rainforest monkeys have very few predators but their main one is the harpy eagle.

This meat-eating predator is the world's largest eagle with a wingspan in excess of two metres! Diving at speeds of up to 50 mph, it grabs and crushes its prey in its deadly talons.

Harpy eagle

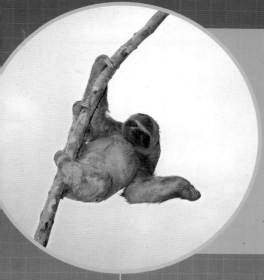

Sloth

Topsy-turvy world

Sloths spend most of their lives upside down in a tree, sleeping up to 18 hours a day! But when they do move, they move incredibly slowly. In fact they move so slowly that sometimes **algae** grows on their fur, turning their greyish brown coat green! They need very little to eat as they do so little.

Did you know?

A sloth's hair grows upside down, so the rain runs off it when it is upside down!

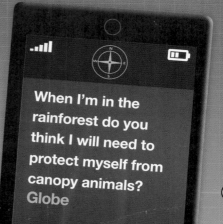

When I'm in the rainforest do you think I will need to protect myself from canopy animals?
Globe

The Understorey

Beneath the canopy

In the dark and steamy understorey you will find many animals that are small and light and can move quickly amongst the trees and vines. Here you will come across lizards, snakes, tree frogs – and thousands of insects!

Hidden

Many lizards in the understorey are coloured green or are able to change their skin colour so they blend in with their surroundings, keeping them safe from predators.

Anole lizards shed their skin every year - and then eat it!

This Amazon anole lizard is green all over except for the males, which have a vent under their throat that turns bright orange when they are threatened or trying to attract a mate. These lizards are **carnivorous** and very **territorial**, and will attack other lizards if they feel threatened.

Instead of using **camouflage** to protect themselves, many tree frogs do exactly the opposite and draw attention to themselves with their brightly coloured skin. The bright colours serve as a warning to other animals that the frog's skin may be poisonous. The golden arrow poison frog, for example, has enough poison in its skin to kill over ten people!

Harlequin poison dart frog

Bugs

Tiny but deadly insects are everywhere in the rainforest. Mosquitoes carry many horrible diseases such as **malaria** and **yellow fever**, both of which can be deadly to humans. In the rainforest, mosquitoes feed on the blood of monkeys but frequently bite humans too.

The rainforest is also home to assassin or kissing bugs which tend to bite their victims at night. They can give humans a nasty illness called Chagas disease. You may not even realise you have the disease until you suddenly die of a heart attack years later!

There are over 2700 different species of mosquito in the world.

Did you know?

Some Amazonian Indians put poison from frogs or plants on their arrow tips when hunting in the forest.

Do you think I am going to have to be more careful near frogs or near insects?

The Forest Floor

Down on the ground

Down on the forest floor there are hundreds of insects and spiders. Many of them, together with fungi and bacteria, are the great recyclers of the rainforest.

Plants get food from the soil. **1**

Some animals eat plants. **2**

Other animals eat these animals. **3**

When animals and plants die they are eaten or broken down by insects, fungi and bacteria and return to the soil as food for plants. **4**

Record breaker

The giant Hercules beetle grows up to 17 cm long. Giant Hercules beetles eat rotting fruit from the forest floor and are mostly active at night.

Did you know?

The giant Hercules beetle is thought to be the strongest creature on Earth for its size, as it can carry up to 850 times its body weight!

Ouch!

The rainforest is teeming with ants. Some march in large armies that swarm over and devour any creature in their path – which must be pretty scary if you are a spider or a scorpion! Humans in the rainforest need to beware of bullet ants. Bullet ants are the largest ants in the world. They also give the nastiest insect sting in the world! The pain can last for 24 hours. Watch out for them between dusk and dawn.

Venomous

Brazilian wandering spiders are not the biggest spiders in the world but they may be one of the most aggressive! This spider does not sit and wait in a web for its prey to come along. It goes out hunting for it instead, especially at night. These spiders are poisonous but when they bite they don't always inject venom into their victims. When they do, their bite can kill. They are not afraid of humans and will attack if they feel threatened.

Did you know?
The sting of a bullet ant is said to be 30 times worse than a wasp sting!

When I'm out walking in the forest at night, which creatures will I need to look out for?
Globe

Did you know?
The Brazilian wandering spider is regarded as the most dangerous spider on Earth!

Rainy season

During the rainy season, the rivers in the Amazon rainforest flood and burst their banks. Low-lying parts of the forest floor are flooded. These forest waterways are inhabited by thousands of different kinds of fish as well as large reptiles like the anaconda. In the dry season, these areas are often home to large land animals such as jaguars.

Powerful predators

Jaguars are the largest cats in South America – they can weigh up to 160 kg and grow to over 2 metres long! They are found in the Amazon rainforest and other parts of South and Central America. Jaguars often live near water and are good swimmers. They are carnivorous and prey on large animals, such as deer. They are very strong animals with powerful jaws and a deadly bite, capable of slicing through the back of their prey's skull and piercing the brain.

The jaguar is the third largest cat, after the tiger and the lion.

Suffocation

Green anacondas are the largest, heaviest snakes in the world. They kill their prey by coiling themselves around their victim and squeezing until it dies of suffocation. No matter how large their victim, an anaconda always swallows its prey whole.

Green anaconda

Killer fish

Piranhas (15–24 cm long) are freshwater fish that live in South American rivers. They have a fearsome reputation for being very aggressive and attacking humans, but this is not really deserved. People who live in the Amazon are happy to swim in piranha-infested rivers in the wet season, when food is plentiful. Piranhas are more likely to attack in the dry season when food is scarce.

Piranhas are carnivorous fish with sharp triangular teeth that can strip their prey down to a skeleton in minutes!

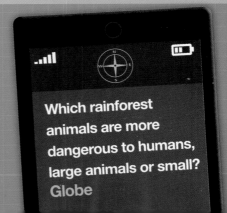

Which rainforest animals are more dangerous to humans, large animals or small?
Globe

DANGEROUS ANIMALS 💀

12th May

I enjoyed reading about the rainforest animals, especially all the creepy-crawlies! I'm beginning to think I might write something about the Amazon rainforest for school. Anyway, it took me ages to decide on my Top Five Most Dangerous Animals in the Rainforest but here they are:

No. 5 ANACONDA

No. 4 JAGUAR

No. 3 MOSQUITO

No. 2 ASSASSIN BUG

But my No 1, to-be-avoided-at-all-costs most dangerous rainforest animal of them all, is <u>THE BRAZILIAN WANDERING SPIDER</u>.

The bad news: territorial
wanders about at night while you sleep
not scared of humans
deadly bite

I scanned this page
and emailed it to Globe.

15th May
Still no reply from Globe.
Hope he hasn't been bitten
by a spider ...

17th May
Globe got back to me at last!

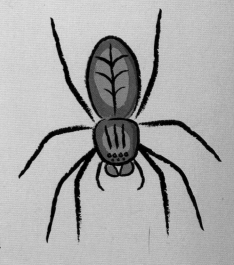

Zac

From: Globetrotter
To: Zac Trotter
Sent: 17th May
Subject: Challenge

Hi Zac,
Sorry to take so long to reply but, until today, we've been deep in the rainforest.

We've *heard* lots of animals, but we've *seen* very few large animals so far. Many of them are way up in the canopy, hidden from view or else only venture out at night. But we have seen tons of small animals: insects, frogs, lizards – and a few snakes!

I can understand why you put the Brazilian wandering spider as your number one dangerous animal, but as long as you check your shoes before putting them on in the morning (as I discovered only yesterday!) you should be okay.

But my number one would be this small but deadly animal – a female Anopheles mosquito. Mosquitoes cause more human deaths than any other creature in the rainforest.

For the final part of your challenge, I want you to find out about the other inhabitants of the rainforest – the people who live and work in the Amazon rainforest and the effect their presence has on the forest.

Will email you again when I can.

Globe

P.S. Reward clue 3: You will need your sleeping bag.

I had thought perhaps I was going on a bat walk for my reward – but now I'm not so sure! I'll just have to finish reading Globe's book …

21

People of the Amazon

Indigenous people

Today, different groups of native peoples live deep in the Amazon rainforest. These groups are the **indigenous** people of the Amazon; people who are **descended from** the very first people who came to live in the forest, thousands of years ago. They live in small, sometimes isolated groups and try to follow a traditional way of life.

Living in harmony

These people know the rainforest better than anyone else and have learned to live in a way that allows them to take everything they need from the forest but without destroying it or doing it any long-lasting harm.

They are very knowledgeable about the plants that grow in the rainforest and gather hundreds of different fruits, nuts, roots and leaves to eat and to use as medicine.

They also build their homes from the materials they find around them. Some tribes also grow crops such as sweet potatoes and beans in small 'gardens' they create in the forest. They are careful to clear just a small area of forest at a time and then let the area **revert** to forest again, before all the goodness has been taken from the soil.

Rainforest people are skilful hunters but they ensure they only take enough animals for their food without endangering the species they hunt.

Under threat

The traditional way of life of these native peoples has been under threat for many years and continues to be under threat today.

Ever since Western and European peoples arrived in South America over 500 years ago, the numbers of indigenous people living in the forest have drastically reduced, as their lands have gradually been taken over and they have died from Western diseases and in violent conflicts over land.

Number of indigenous people living in the Amazon

1500	1900	Today
6 to 9 million	1 million	250 000 or fewer

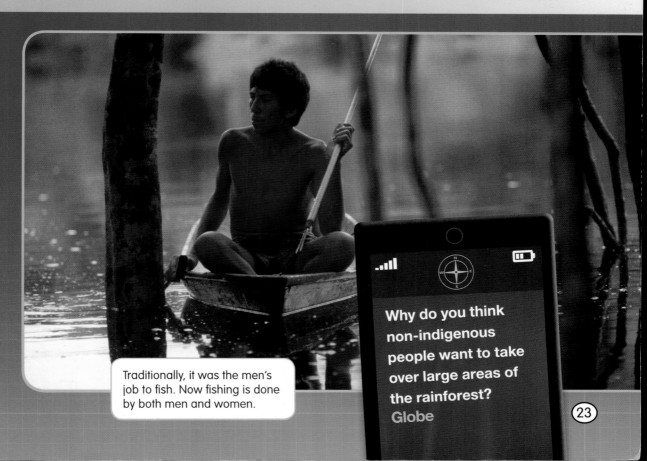

Traditionally, it was the men's job to fish. Now fishing is done by both men and women.

Why do you think non-indigenous people want to take over large areas of the rainforest?
Globe

Industry

Natural resources

Rainforests are home to many precious **natural resources** such as wood, minerals, rubber, food and medicines. Many people are keen to **exploit** these resources and make money from them. As a result, more and more rainforest is being turned over to industry every year. But in order to make way for this industry, large parts of the rainforest have had to be cut down. This is called deforestation.

Causes of deforestation in Brazilian Amazon 2000–2005	
Cattle ranching	65–70 %
Settlers' farms	20–25 %
Large farms	5–10 %
Logging	2–3 %
Mining (and others)	1–2 %

Find it!

Which is the bigger cause of deforestation in the Amazon rainforest, farming or ranching?

Timber-rrrr!

There is great demand for wood in the world, both for building and for making charcoal and paper. Since the rainforest's greatest resource is its trees, **logging** companies have for many years been building roads deep into the Amazon forest and cutting down trees to sell. Unfortunately when they cut down the trees, the rest of the plants in the area soon die as they are no longer protected by the canopy of trees.

Farming

There is also a huge demand throughout the world for cheap meat. Farmers have been clearing huge areas of rainforest to use as grazing land for their cattle and to grow crops like soya on a large scale.

As well as ranchers and farmers, many poor settlers are moving into the forest from the surrounding cities and towns, looking for a place to live and to grow their own food.

However, after several harvests, farming robs the rainforest soil of its nutrients, so farmers then have to move on and cut down *more* forest for a new farm or ranch.

Amazon gold is mined from large open pits.

Gold!

Many rainforests around the world are rich in precious metals and stones. Gold, diamonds, lead and copper have all been found in the Amazon rainforest in the past few years. Large areas of forest have been cleared to set up the mines and unfortunately some of these mines have also been responsible for polluting the surrounding soil and rivers.

There are about 100 000 cattle ranches in the Amazon rainforest.

Can you think of at least two ways that industry has affected the rainforest?
Globe

Impact

In danger

Left alone, rainforests grow into a rich environment where trees, plants and animals all live together happily. Rainforests work well because every living thing in the forest depends on every other living thing in the forest for its survival. Remove one thing from the rainforest (such as the trees) and it affects the whole forest, endangering the lives of its plants, its animals and its people.

Rainforest facts

● 2000 trees a minute are being cut down in the rainforest.

● More than a hundred species of plants and animals are being lost every day.

● If this carries on, there may be little or no rainforest left in 50 years' time.

Rainforest is often burned like this, to clear the ground for farming.

Deep in debt

Our planet's rainforests are in some of the poorest countries in the world. Many of these countries have big debts. For countries in this situation, bringing industry into the forest is seen as a quick way for governments to make money to help them pay off their debts.

Solving the problem

Ideally, what is needed is a *lasting* way for poor countries to make the money they need from their rainforests, *but without destroying the forests forever!*

One idea that may work is for the forest to be left standing and for its many *renewable* resources such as fruits, nuts, rubber, chocolate and medicinal plants to be harvested, instead. This way:

● money will be earned by selling these products

● the rainforest will continue to produce these for years to come

● damage to the forest will be minimal.

Once an area of forest has been cleared of its timber, it takes years to re-grow. Even then, it will not grow back as it was. Once lost, rainforest is often lost for ever.

Why do you think governments don't do more to stop the rainforest from disappearing?
Globe

REWARD

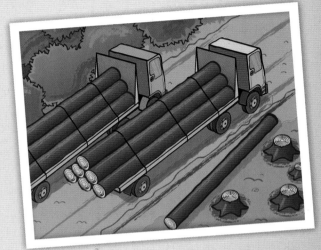

2nd June

It was over a fortnight before I heard from Globe again, when he emailed this photo he had taken in the rainforest.

I told him I was horrified by what I had read about all the industry in the rainforest and by the photos he had sent me of the deforestation that he had come across in the Amazon. Globe is very worried about the impact deforestation is having on the rainforest too and when I said that perhaps the most dangerous thing in the rainforest was people rather than mosquitoes, he said he thought I had successfully completed his challenge!

He was pleased to hear that I was going to find out even more about the rainforest so I could write about the destruction of the rainforest for my school project.

He's sent me details of my reward — two places for me and Dad on a Sleepover Safari at the City Zoo, as soon as my leg is out of plaster. I can't wait!

28th June

Going on the Sleepover Safari at the zoo must be one of the most amazing things I've ever done! We got to the zoo just as it was getting dark and met up with all the other people on the sleepover in the invertebrate house, where we were going to sleep for the night. One of the keepers brought in a huge tarantula for us to see up close. It was as big as her hand!

scorpion

Then we went for a walk around the zoo in the dark. You really notice the sounds the animals make at night and it was weird seeing animals like tigers and lions by torchlight.

bush baby

After that we went to sleep in the invertebrate room. Not that we slept a lot, surrounded by spiders, beetles and scorpions! In the morning, we had a chance to look inside the rainforest house. Amazingly I got to see sloths and monkeys just like the ones Globe had sent me photos of. It was good to see that the zoo was helping to keep these endangered animals alive.

bat

DANGER

30th June

This is the written work about the rainforest that I wrote for school.

Today, Miss Williams said I could take it home to put in my journal, so I could show it to Uncle Globe when he comes home next week ...

Danger in the Rainforest
By Zac Trotter

Lots of amazing, often rare, animals live in the rainforest. Some are deadly and dangerous both to other animals and to humans. But there is something even more dangerous in the rainforest than jaguars and mosquitoes and they are the people who live and work in the forest.

For years, the indigenous people who live quietly in the rainforest without harming it, have watched in horror as logging, mining, farming and ranching activities have begun to destroy the world they know. Trees that have taken hundreds of years to grow are being cut down and not replaced. Mile after mile of rainforest is being burned or cut down.

Hyacinth macaw
Endangered due to loss of habitat and the illegal pet trade.

Did you know that rainforests used to cover 14% of the earth's surface and that now they barely cover 6%? Did you know that every day more and more species of animal and plants disappear from the rainforest, never to return?

Some of the biggest threats to the rainforest animals are loss of habitat, pollution and poaching; **all of which are caused by humans!** This has meant that many other animals and plants, though still living in the rainforest, are now endangered.

The rainforest is important to everyone living on Earth, not just to endangered animals and plants, as it helps to keep the Earth's climate in balance. It does this by storing and recycling vast quantities of rainwater. The trees and plants absorb the carbon dioxide we exhale and release the oxygen we need to breathe.

The rainforest is vital to us all, so we all need to help find ways to protect it. Remember: only humans have destroyed it and only humans can save it.

Three-toed sloth
Homes destroyed by farming and logging.

Jaguar
Homes destroyed by industry and the big cats hunted for their fur.

Glossary

algae simple plants without roots, stems or leaves

camouflage the colour of an animal that allows it to blend in with its surroundings

canopy like a roof

carnivorous meat-eating

descended from related to people from a long time ago

equator imaginary line around the middle of Earth

exploit to make money from something

humid warm and damp

indigenous the people who first settled in a place or territory

logging cutting forest timber

malaria dangerous illness with high fever, that can be life-threatening

natural resources things that grow or occur naturally that can be sold

nutrients goodness, food

orchid flowering plant

revert to return, go back

species type, kind of animal or plant

submerged under water

territorial will defend their own space

yellow fever disease spread by mosquitoes that can be life-threatening

Index